my feelings

When I'm Angry...

Moira Butterfield

Published in paperback in 2016
First published in 2014 by Wayland
© Wayland 2014

Wayland, an imprint of Hachette Children's Group
Part of Hodder & Stoughton
Carmelite House, 50 Victoria Embankment, London EC4Y 0DZ

Produced for Wayland by
White-Thomson Publishing Ltd
www.wtpub.co.uk
+44 (0) 843 208 7460

Editor: Stephen White-Thomson
Design: Rocket Design (East Anglia) Ltd

A catalogue for this title is available from the British Library

ISBN: 978 0 7502 8968 9
Library e-book ISBN: 978 0 7502 9126 2
Dewey Number: 152.4'7-dc23

10 9 8 7 6 5 4 3 2 1

Wayland is a division of Hachette Children's Books,
an Hachette UK company.
www.hachette.co.uk

Printed and bound in China

Picture credits:
Crossley: 8; Shutterstock.com: Gelpi JM 4, ollyy 5, ffoto29 6, paffy
7, holbox 9, Luis Louro 10, Andresr 11, Linn Currie 12, picturepartners
13, Nina Buday 14, MidoSemsem 15, Steven Leon Day 16 - 17, Tracy
Whiteside 18, Inga Marchuk 19, Warren Goldswain 20, Samuel Borges
Photography 21.

When I'm angry I might...

explode like a volcano...

stomp like a dinosaur...

bellow like an elephant...

I need a HUG!

Take a look and see...

What a **fierce frown!**
My eyebrows and my mouth go down.

You can see I'm angry.

I feel as if
I might
explode.

I'm like a
volcano
about to
blow!

BOOM!

5

My angry face could scare the **scariest monsters...**

Grrrr!

...and frighten the **fiercest pirates.**

Watch out!

Sometimes, if I do something silly, I get angry with myself.

I stamp my feet

like a fierce dinosaur...

STOMP!

...and I **bellow** as loudly as an elephant!

Aaarrrghhhh!

9

Then my mum
gives me
a hug.

It chases away **my angry feelings,** like the sun chases storm clouds away.

If my dog chews my shoes,

I lose my temper.

I act like a **grumpy gorilla!**

But if I take time out, and sit very quietly...

Sssshhhhhh!

14

...I can make
my temper

disappear
like magic.

Shazam!

My sister sometimes gets **angry** with me, and I get **mad** with her.

We both fold
our arms and
look fed up.

But then it feels good to say
"SORRY" to each other so...

...our angry feelings

float away,

just like balloons.

Bye bye!

So now I know three ways to stop feeling angry:

hugging,

sitting quietly,

and saying sorry.

One, Two, Three!

Smile! (It's a lot easier.)

Do it!

Pretend to stamp your feet and wave your arms like a **grumpy gorilla.**

Now can you make a **happy face?**

Can you make a face angry enough to **scare a monster?**

Now pretend to dance around like a **happy gorilla.**

Stamp your feet like a fierce dinosaur.

STOMP!

Show me a **fierce frown!**

Can you bellow like an **elephant?**

Take some time out, and sit very quietly...

23

Teacher's and parent's notes:

These books are designed for children to explore feelings in a fun interactive way. Encourage them to have fun pointing to the pictures, making sounds and doing some acting, too.

During or after your reading, you could encourage your child to talk further about their own feelings, if they want to. Here are some conversation prompts to try:

Can you remember a time when you felt angry?

Can you think of a good way to stop feeling angry?

Activities to try:

✳ On a piece of paper, draw or paint some angry faces or angry-looking monsters.

✳ On a piece of paper, draw your favourite picture from this book

Further reading:

Dinosaurs Have Feelings, Too: Anna Angrysaurus,
written by Brian Moses and illustrated by Mike Gordon (Wayland, 2013)

You Choose! Don't Get Angry, Annie,
written by Lisa Regan and illustrated by Alice Busby (Wayland, 2014)

Your Emotions: I Feel Angry,
written by Brian Moses and illustrated by Mike Gordon (Wayland)